Louis Pasteur

Disease Detective

Michael Webb

Copp Clark Pitman Ltd.
A Longman Company

ISBN 0-7730-5158-9 (Casebound) ISBN 0-7730-5159-7 (Paperback)

Canadian Cataloguing in Publication Data
Webb, Michael, 1949–
Louis Pasteur, disease detective

(Scientists & inventors series) Includes index.
ISBN 0-7730-5158-9 (bound) ISBN 0-7730-5159-7 (pbk.)

1. Pasteur, Louis, 1822–1895 — Juvenile literature. 2. Scientists — France — Biography — Juvenile literature. 3. Chemists — France — Biography — Juvenile literature. 4. Microbiologists — France — Biography — Juvenile literature. I. Title. II. Series.

Q143.P2W4 1991 j509.2 C91-094534-9

MICHAEL WEBB, a former school teacher and chemistry professor, now works as an editor and writer in Toronto. He has a doctorate in chemistry from the University of Alberta.

EDITING AND PHOTO RESEARCH: *Melanie Sherwood*
SERIES DESIGN: *Susan Hedley*
LAYOUT AND ART DIRECTION: *Liz Nyman*
TYPESETTING: *Sonja Mills Graphic Arts Inc.*
PRINTING AND BINDING: *Friesen Printers Ltd.*

ACKNOWLEDGEMENTS
Special thanks to Francesca Verre, aged 12, to Paolo Verre, aged 9, and to Grace D'Alfonso for reading the manuscript.

PHOTO AND ILLUSTRATION CREDITS
Canadian Dairy Commission: 25; *Canapress:* 1, 15, 20, 23; *Connaught Laboratories Limited:* 21; *Malcolm Cullen:* 4, 22; *French Government Tourist Office:* 6; *IMS Creative Communications:* 12; *Mary Evans Picture Library:* 9; *Ministry of Agriculture and Food, Ottawa:* 16; *The Ontario Milk Marketing Board:* 24; *Pasteur Institute:* cover, iv, 2, 3, 7, 8, 10, 13, 14, 17, 18, 19; *Royal Ontario Museum, Department of Minerology:* 5; *Tetra Brik:* 11.

Copp Clark Pitman Ltd., 2775 Matheson Blvd. East, Mississauga, Ontario L4W 4P7
Printed and bound in Canada.

2 3 4 5 5158-9 00 99 98
1 2 3 4 5 5159-7 95 94 93 92 91

CONTENTS

Louis Pasteur.

Introduction

If you look closely at a carton of milk, you will see the word "pasteurized." This word tells you that the milk has been processed in a way that makes it safe for you to drink. The word "pasteurized" comes from the name of one of the greatest scientists who ever lived, Louis Pasteur.

Pasteur did not just work out how to process milk. In the entire history of science, very few have achieved as much as Pasteur. He made great medical discoveries about how diseases spread and how we can fight them. His work has saved millions and millions of lives.

You will see the word "pasteurized" on milk cartons.

Early Years

On December 22, 1822, Louis Pasteur was born in Dôle, a small town in Eastern France. He grew up in nearby Arbois, where his father ran a **tannery**. Louis's mother kept the **accounts** of the business. His family wanted Louis to be a professor, so he was expected to do well in school.

Louis had three sisters. He was the second oldest of the children. He was a quiet, serious boy. Though he was a good student, he did not seem brilliant. He always worked slowly and carefully.

Louis Pasteur was born in this house.

Young Louis liked playing with his friends, and loved fishing. He was very good at drawing and painting. As a teenager, he thought about becoming an artist. He drew many portraits of his friends and relatives with coloured chalks.

Louis went to college in Besançon, about 40 kilometres from home. By the time he was 17, he was losing interest in drawing and painting. He read a lot of **literature**, but his strongest interest was in science. He wanted to study it at a very famous school, the École Normale Supérieure. This meant moving to Paris, the capital of France. But the school was hard to get into, and Louis was still not an outstanding student.

Louis drew these portraits of his parents.

Paris

Louis lived in different parts of France.

At age 19, Louis took the exams for a place at the École Normale. He did not do that well and wanted to study for another year. He set off for Paris to study at a boarding school. He paid part of the cost by helping younger students with their math. That year, Louis also took some classes in **chemistry** at the Sorbonne, a university in Paris.

Louis had a good friend in Paris, Charles Chappuis. Louis and Charles enjoyed eating out, and went to the theatre and the opera. Louis's work went well. He got his place at the École Normale. He studied chemistry and **physics** there.

Louis began to do **research** on **crystals**. He was fascinated by their shapes and their effect on light. His parents worried that Louis might be working too hard and might ruin his health. But Louis's research went well. By August, 1847, he had completed his **doctorate**.

Dr. Louis Pasteur carried on with his research. But he had little money and needed a job. At the end of 1848, he became a professor in Dijon. Teaching took up all of his time. He was sad that he could not do research. So, within a few months, he moved to the University of Strasbourg.

Louis loved to study crystals.

Marie

Pasteur reached Strasbourg on January 15, 1849. He was 26 years old. He soon met the head of the University, Professor Laurent, and fell in love with one of his daughters, Marie. Their wedding took place on May 29, 1849. The Pasteurs soon started a family.

Marie began to learn all about Louis's work. She read a lot about research. She began to work as Louis's secretary. Marie often wrote out Louis's articles that he sent to be published in science journals. She sometimes helped out with experiments. Pasteur knew he was lucky to have found Marie.

Strasbourg.

Marie Pasteur later in her life.

Though he had a good job and a happy marriage, Pasteur was not satisfied. His **laboratory** in Strasbourg was poor, and he needed more money for research. So, the Pasteurs moved again, this time to the University of Lille in 1854. Louis was 32 years old and already well-known for his work on crystals. In fact, in 1853, he had received an important award, called the Legion of Honour.

Many factories around Lille made **alcohol** from sugar beets in a process called **fermentation**. In 1856, Pasteur had a visit from a factory owner. His alcohol was spoiling, and he did not know why. At that time, no one knew how fermentation worked. Pasteur looked at samples of the fermenting sugar under a microscope. He soon started to see a pattern.

Pasteur found that these microbes spoiled wine.
This is what he saw through his microscope.

To make the sugar ferment faster, workers added **yeast** to it. No one knew exactly what yeast was. Pasteur shocked everyone by saying that yeast was actually alive and feeding on the sugar! We now think of yeast as a very simple kind of plant.

But Pasteur saw something even more important. There were other tiny living things in the samples. Scientists call them "microbes." The common name for them is "germs." Pasteur found that, if there were microbes in the fermenting sugar, the alcohol went bad. If there were no microbes, the alcohol was fine. So, the way to make good alcohol was to keep microbes out.

Pasteur also studied milk. He found that microbes make milk go sour. But the microbes he found in milk looked different from the ones in fermenting sugar.

In 1857, Pasteur moved back to the École Normale in Paris. There, over the next 20 years, he studied vinegar, wine, and beer. All of them are made by fermentation, and all of them can spoil. Pasteur found that a different microbe could spoil each liquid. It seemed that one microbe could do only one job.

Where the microbes came from was a mystery. Some scientists thought that microbes could form from non-living material. Others thought that living microbes must have come from other living microbes, like you come from living parents.

Paris looked like this when Pasteur lived there.

Hunting for Microbes

To find out which idea was right, Pasteur first looked for microbes in the air. He drew air through a little plug of cotton wool to catch anything floating around in it. He also kept air away from liquids, like milk, that usually went bad. As long as he kept the air out, the liquids did not spoil. But the liquids spoiled if he put a little of the cotton wool in them. He realized that he had trapped microbes from the air in the cotton wool.

Pasteur found no evidence that microbes could just come to life. They had to arrive from somewhere and then multiply. So, canned, bottled, and **vacuum-packed** foods keep well for the reason Pasteur discovered. If there are no microbes in them, and none are allowed to get in, the foods do not go bad.

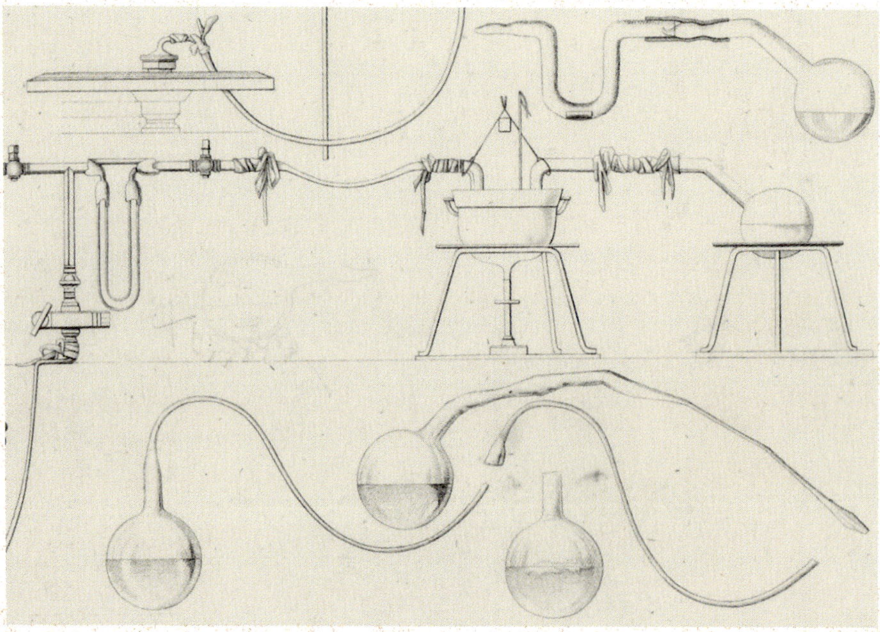

Pasteur's sketches of some of his equipment.

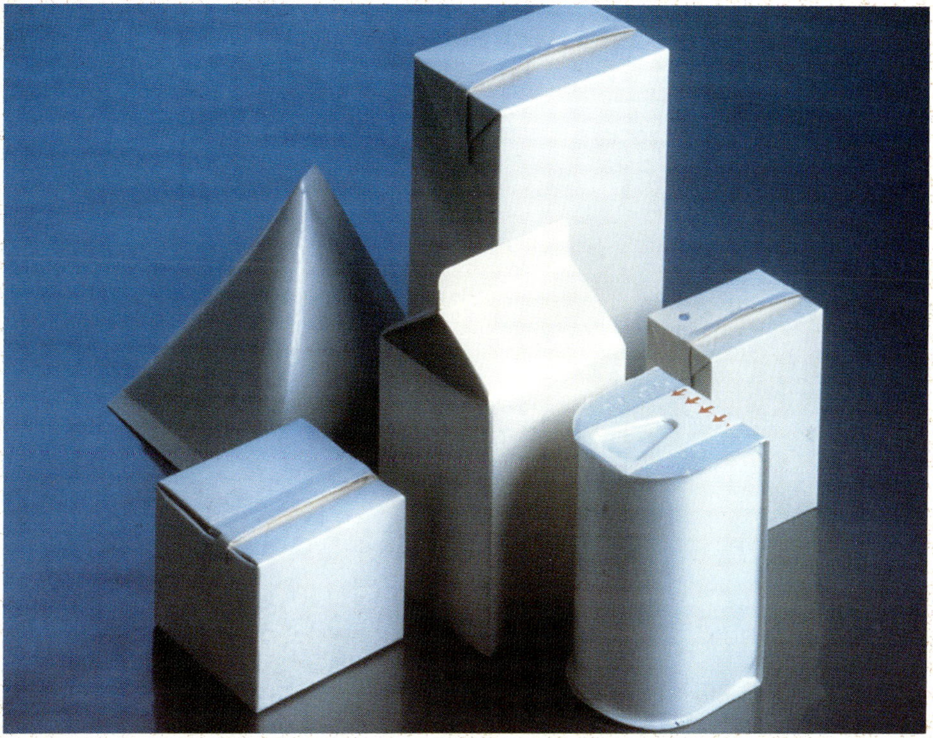

These modern packages keep microbes out of food.

Because microbes are so tiny and float around in the air, it is hard to keep them out of things. Pasteur wanted a way of killing microbes that were already inside something. People knew that food could be kept by cooking and canning it, but strong heating changes some foods a lot. Think of the smell and taste of boiled milk, compared with fresh milk.

Pasteur found that he could kill the microbes in wine by heating it for a short time to about 55 to 60 degrees Celcius. (This is about as hot as the water from a hot-water tap.) Unlike boiling, this gentler heating did not ruin the taste or smell of the wine. People started calling this way of killing microbes "pasteurization." It was soon used on milk, vinegar, beer, and other foods and drinks.

Diseases

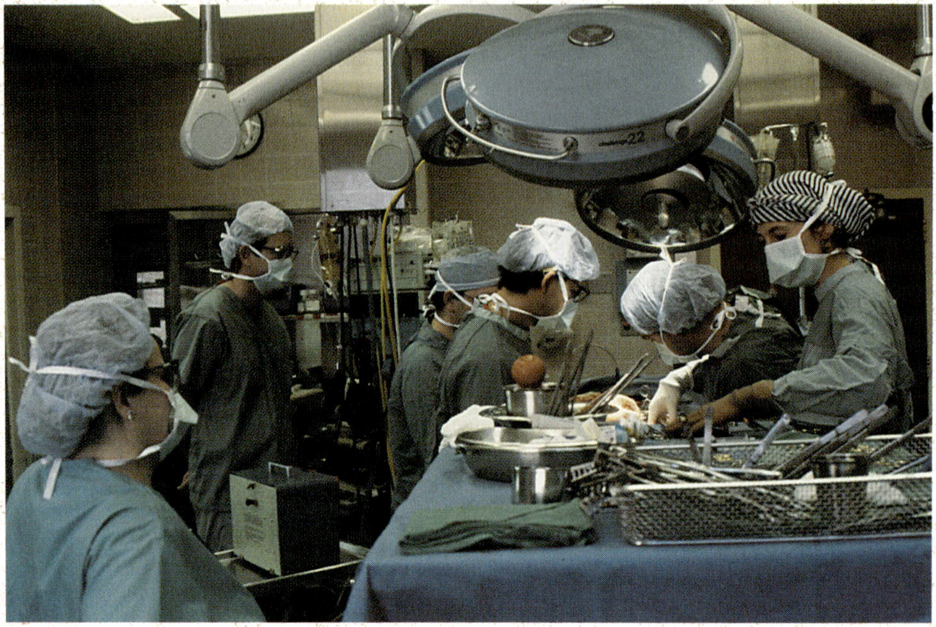

Surgeons try to keep germs out of wounds.

While working on fermentation and thinking about microbes, Pasteur had an idea that changed the world. People knew that some diseases could pass from one person to another, but no one knew exactly what spread them. Pasteur had the idea that microbes might spread diseases. We call his idea the "germ theory" of disease.

Joseph Lister, an English **surgeon**, heard about Pasteur's germ theory in 1864. Lister found ways to keep germs out of wounds during surgery. Some ways were quite simple. He told surgeons to wash their hands, and to use bandages and equipment that were clean, so that they had no germs on them. The number of people who died from infections after surgery soon fell.

A silkworm feeding on mulberry leaves.

In 1865, Pasteur began research on diseases himself. A big industry in France was the making of silk. The silk industry had millions and millions of **silkworms**. A disease was killing them. Pasteur agreed to help, though he knew nothing at all about silkworms. He found that some of the worms' parents, adult moths, were passing on a microbe. His solution was to use only worms from healthy moths. He saved the silk industry.

Though he was successful, Pasteur's life was not easy. Over a period of 20 years, his parents and three of his five children had died, and Louis himself became ill. In October, 1868, he had a **stroke**. It paralysed his left side. Three months after the stroke, he was back at work. But for the rest of his life, his left hand was stiff, and he walked with a limp.

Research on Farm Animals

Louis Pasteur in his laboratory.

By 1877, Pasteur was studying anthrax. This disease killed many thousands of farm animals every year. It also killed some people, like farmers and butchers, who worked with them. A famous German scientist, Robert Koch, discovered a microbe that he thought caused anthrax, but he could not prove it. Pasteur did.

Pasteur next studied another disease in animals, chicken cholera. He grew chicken cholera microbes and proved that he could use them to give chickens the disease. But then came a lucky accident. He left some microbes around for a few weeks over the summer, instead of using them right away. He found that the hens he tested them on did not die. So he tried a fresh batch of the microbe on the same chickens. They still did not die.

Pasteur realized that the old microbes, which had weakened over the summer, could not kill the chickens. But the weakened microbes had made the chickens **immune** to the fresh microbes. He had found a way of **vaccinating** chickens against the disease!

Pasteur soon developed a **vaccine** against anthrax. Again, he used a weakened form of the microbe. He tested it on sheep, cows, oxen, and goats. It worked — he could protect them against the disease.

Finally, he tackled swine fever. This disease killed tens of thousands of pigs in France and other countries. Over a million had died in the U.S. alone in 1879. Again, Pasteur developed a vaccine.

Pasteur developed vaccines to protect farm animals against diseases.

Saving People

In 1880, Pasteur began to study another animal disease, called rabies. Because the microbe that caused it was very small, Pasteur could not find it with his microscope. But he could grow the microbe in rabbits, then dry it to weaken it. This gave him his vaccine.

Rabies affected people as well as animals. People mainly got the disease through bites from **infected** dogs and wolves. It could take weeks or months for rabies to develop after a bite. So Pasteur tried his vaccine on dogs that had already been bitten by dogs with rabies. The vaccine worked as long as no signs of the disease had appeared. Once these signs appeared, the disease always caused death.

Today, dogs can be vaccinated against rabies.

Dr. Edward Jenner.

Though Pasteur wanted to prevent rabies in humans, he was very nervous about doing experiments on people. Until then, there was only one vaccine for humans, and no one understood why it worked. It protected against a disease called "smallpox." The vaccine was discovered in England about 90 years earlier by a doctor named Edward Jenner.

Jenner knew that people who worked with cows often got a milder disease called "cowpox." But few of these people seemed to get smallpox. Jenner found that he could vaccinate people against smallpox by giving them cowpox on purpose. In fact, it was Jenner who made up the word "vaccination." It comes from the Latin word *vacca*, which means "cow."

Final Years

On July 6, 1885, a nine year-old boy, Joseph Meister, was brought to Pasteur. A dog with rabies had bitten Joseph two days before. He was likely to die without help. Pasteur tried vaccinating him. The vaccine worked, and Joseph Meister lived for another 55 years! Soon, hundreds of people were coming to Pasteur for vaccination against rabies.

But, by the time he helped Joseph Meister, Pasteur's health was beginning to suffer from all his hours of work. He rarely did anything else. There were signs of a heart problem.

Louis Pasteur's 70th birthday was a grand occasion.

In 1892, Pasteur celebrated his 70th birthday. It was a grand occasion, held at the Sorbonne. The President of the French Republic was there. So were leading scientists from many countries. Joseph Lister, the great surgeon who had used Pasteur's ideas, gave one of the speeches. By then, Pasteur's voice was weak, so his son read his speech for him.

Louis Pasteur died on September 28, 1895, at the age of 72. His name lives on through the Pasteur Institute, which he opened in Paris in 1888. At first, its main purpose was to vaccinate people at risk of rabies. It has since become world famous for its research into diseases. Many vaccines are made there.

The Pasteur Institute.

Friendly Microbes

By now, you may think that microbes are quite nasty. They can ruin valuable products, like milk and wine, and can cause some horrible diseases. But Pasteur found that it takes a certain microbe to do a certain job. If we find a microbe that does what we want, it can work for us, not against us.

There are, in fact, many useful microbes. We depend on them to deal with **sewage**, for example. Towns and cities have sewage treatment plants, in which "friendly" microbes break down sewage. They make it safer to pump sewage into rivers and lakes. In the country, many houses have **septic tanks**, in which microbes also help destroy sewage.

Making microbes today.

Alexander Fleming.

Some microbes kill other microbes. So we can use some microbes to make drugs. These drugs kill other microbes that cause diseases. The drugs that microbes make are called “antibiotics.” A Scottish doctor, Alexander Fleming, discovered the first one in 1928. He called it “penicillin.” It is still a very important drug. Many other drugs now come from microbes.

There are even microbes around that chew on rocks! Some mining companies use these microbes to get the valuable metals copper and **uranium** out of the ground.

We do not have to rely on natural microbes to help us. Scientists now have ways of making new microbes. So the number of jobs they can do for us keeps getting bigger and bigger.

Getting Your Shots

You have probably been vaccinated against quite a few diseases, including diphtheria, whooping cough, and polio. If you travel to other countries, especially to very hot ones, you may need other shots. One possibility is a shot for yellow fever.

There are still many diseases for which there is no vaccine. One is the common cold. Another is a very serious disease for millions of people around the world — malaria. So we still need a lot more research.

This type of mosquito carries malaria.

Rabies has existed in Canada for at least 170 years. The first recorded case killed the Canadian Governor-in-Chief, the Duke of Richmond, in 1819. Though few people now get rabies in Canada, it is still common in animals. Southern Ontario is the worst area for rabies in all of North America. Most reported cases in Canada occur in foxes, skunks, and cattle.

Pet dogs and cats should be vaccinated against rabies. As Pasteur discovered all those years ago, people can be saved from the disease by shots given after they are bitten. People who work with animals a lot, like veterinarians, can have shots ahead of time.

Some foxes and skunks have rabies.

The Dairy Industry

If Pasteur had done nothing except work on milk, his findings would still be very valuable. There are over two million dairy cows in Canada! Between them, they produce over seven billion (7 000 000 000) litres of milk a year!

The dairy industry gives a perfect example of how microbes can harm us or help us. As Pasteur found, microbes cause milk to spoil. That is why pasteurization is so important. These days, trucks collect fresh milk from dairy farms and take it to large processing plants for pasteurization.

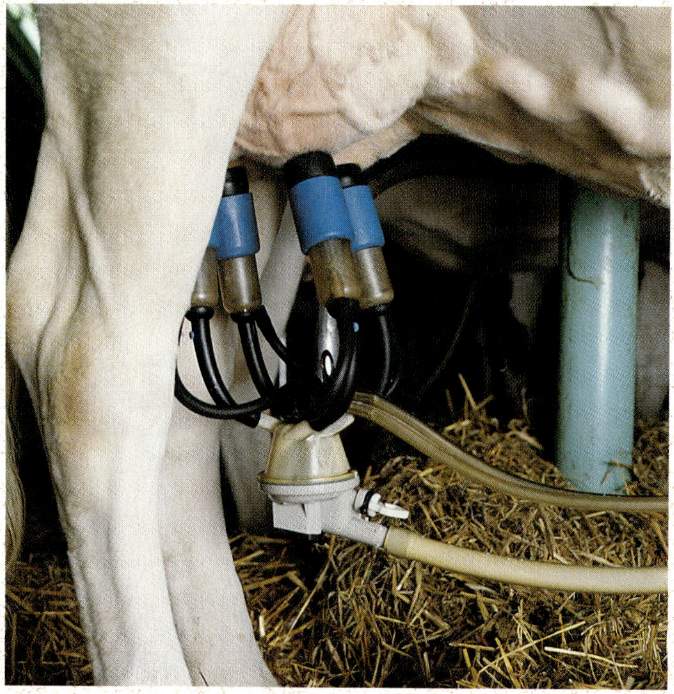

On modern farms, cows are milked by machine.

Microbes turn milk into cheese.

Though killing some microbes is good for milk production, other microbes are added to some milk. Microbes turn milk into yoghurt, cheese, cottage cheese, and buttermilk. Microbes also turn cream into sour cream.

So the next time you eat or drink a dairy product, take an antibiotic for an illness, or have a vaccination, perhaps you will think about the good and bad side of microbes. And maybe the name Louis Pasteur will cross your mind. In the history of science, there are few who can compare with him.

GLOSSARY

accounts — Lists of the money made and spent by a business. *(p. 2)*

alcohol — A colourless liquid with many uses, including beer, wine, and some medicines. Alcohol is even mixed with gasoline to run some cars. *(p. 7)*

chemistry — The study of changes in which materials are changed into other materials. (An example is the study of a wood fire, which changes wood into ash and smoke.) *(p. 4)*

crystals — Glittery chunks. (Table salt, sugar, and diamonds are examples of crystals.) *(p. 5)*

doctorate — The highest degree a person can study for in a university. A person working for a doctorate does **research**. *(p. 5)*

fermentation — A way of changing one material into another (sugar into **alcohol**, for example). *(p. 7)*

immune — Unable to get a disease. *(p. 15)*

infected — Having a disease or illness. (If you have a cold, you are infected with the germs that cause it.) *(p. 16)*

laboratory — A room where scientists do experiments. *(p. 7)*

literature — Stories and poems by great writers. *(p. 3)*

physics — The study of certain features of the world around us, such as light, sound, electricity, and how things move. *(p. 4)*

research – Work done to find out and explain new facts. *(p. 5)*

septic tanks – Underground tanks, in which microbes break down **sewage.** *(p. 20)*

sewage – Waste water, including waste from household sinks and toilets. *(p. 20)*

silkworms – Small worms that make silk. *(p. 13)*

stroke – An injury to the brain caused by a broken or blocked blood vessel. (A blood vessel is a tube that carries blood around the body.) *(p. 13)*

surgeon – A doctor who treats diseases and injuries by operating on people. (If you have had your appendix or tonsils removed, the work was done by a surgeon.) *(p. 12)*

tannery – A business that makes animal skins into leather. *(p. 2)*

uranium – An important metal, used to make electricity in nuclear reactors. *(p. 21)*

vaccinating – Giving someone a **vaccine** to protect against a disease. *(p. 15)*

vaccine – Something a doctor can give a person to prevent a disease. Many vaccines are injected with needles. *(p. 15)*

vacuum-packed – Sealed in a container with no air in it. There are many vacuum-packed products, including instant coffee. *(p. 10)*

yeast – A yellow powder that causes **fermentation.** (Yeast is commonly used to ferment bread and make it rise during baking.) *(p. 8)*

INDEX

Harriett Todd Public School

George Street, Orillia, Ont. L3V 2V1 (705) 325-9388